Enes Cinko

The (continued) employment of employees who are entitled to a pension

Enes Cinko

The (continued) employment of employees who are entitled to a pension

as a way out of staff shortages

ScienciaScripts

Imprint
Any brand names and product names mentioned in this book are subject to trademark, brand or patent protection and are trademarks or registered trademarks of their respective holders. The use of brand names, product names, common names, trade names, product descriptions etc. even without a particular marking in this work is in no way to be construed to mean that such names may be regarded as unrestricted in respect of trademark and brand protection legislation and could thus be used by anyone.

Cover image: www.ingimage.com

This book is a translation from the original published under ISBN 978-620-2-21559-6.

Publisher:
Sciencia Scripts
is a trademark of
Dodo Books Indian Ocean Ltd. and OmniScriptum S.R.L publishing group

120 High Road, East Finchley, London, N2 9ED, United Kingdom
Str. Armeneasca 28/1, office 1, Chisinau MD-2012, Republic of Moldova, Europe
Managing Directors: Ieva Konstantinova, Victoria Ursu
info@omniscriptum.com

Printed at: see last page
ISBN: 978-620-7-80631-7

Summary

The aim of this Bachelor's thesis is to find out whether and how employees entitled to a pension can continue to be employed in order to counteract staff shortages. The new regulation of § 41 sentence 3 SGB VI is already seen as a way out in many companies, but from a legal point of view it is associated with a high risk and ideally needs to be amended again by the legislator. On the one hand, the work process consists of analysing and interpreting legal texts. This thesis also drafted a model for companies to avoid the risks of Section 41 sentence 3. On the other hand, the Bremen Regional Labour Court provides a practical example of the risks associated with § 41 sentence 3 SGB VI. Advantages, disadvantages and suggestions for improving the provision round off the thesis. In addition, various opinions were included in order to present a variety of perspectives on the planned law.

Table of Contents

Chapter 1

1 Introduction

"Growing old is like climbing a mountain. The higher you get, the more energy you use up, but the further you can see." Ingmar Bergmann[1]

This quote from Ingmar Bergmann expresses the importance of pensionable employees in the world of work. Although their strength gradually diminishes over time, these workers nevertheless have the greatest wealth of experience and should be regarded as valuable resources for the labour market. For some years now, the terms "staff shortage" or "skills shortage" have been heard in the labour market in connection with certain professions. This thesis essentially focusses on two aspects. Firstly, it looks at the economic and demographic causes, which are described in more detail in chapters 2 and 3. The causes, reasons and future forecasts regarding the labour shortage are discussed.
The second focus is on the legal solutions that could serve as a way out of these bottlenecks. Section 41 sentence 3 SGB VI and section 14 TzBfG, which are discussed in chapter 5, are decisive here. Chapter 6.3 discusses the gaps and risks associated with this newly introduced provision. This is underpinned later in the thesis by the case of the LAG Bremen. It is concluded that the legislator must make changes to this new regulation, especially as it is not legal in the context of European law. However, the question also arises on the part of companies: What can I do as a company/employer to (continue to) employ employees entitled to a pension or to continue to utilise this capacity? Chapter 6.4 presents a draft contract that we have drawn up ourselves. This utilises both provisions and thus provides a template that employers could use. Finally, Chapter 7 offers further alternative proposals that companies could use to utilise the capacities and experience of older workers in the long term. Finally, in the conclusion, a subjective statement is made on the overall topic and the results.

1.1 Problem definition

Chancellor Angela Merkel has already described it quite well: "[...] If we in Germany become fewer, older and more diverse in the long term, this will have an impact on both young and old, on people in the cities and in the countryside, on employees and employers".[2] It is undisputed that major changes

[1] Swedish screenwriter (2011), http://www.kunst-des-altems.de/zitate/, (last accessed on: 06/06/2017).

[2] See Press and Information Office of the Federal Government (2017), (https://www.bundesregierung.de/ContentArchiv/DE/Archiv17/Interview/2013/08/2013-08-08-merkel-ula.html) , (last

will occur over time, which go hand in hand with the constant change in German demographics. According to the Federal Agency for Civic Education (bpb), life expectancy in Germany has been rising continuously since the mid-1970s, while the birth rate continues to fall. This can also be proven statistically. In this respect, the proportion of the population aged under 20 fell by almost ten per cent between 1960 and 2011, while the proportion of people aged 60 and over rose by almost ten per cent.[3] This ongoing demographic change is ultimately leading to a further reduction in the number of people in employment. In addition, the number of unqualified school leavers is increasing, which in turn leads to growing staff shortages and a lack of skilled labour. As a result of this vicious circle, many employers[4] are increasingly focussing on older employees involuntarily. The result is longer employment or re-employment. Although some employers are considering or already employing[5] retirees, the majority of companies and employers continue to associate them with negative characteristics and therefore avoid them.[6] In some cases, these can be very different characteristics. Insufficient motivation, a slower work process and the fear that too great an age difference among colleagues could lead to conflicts and discrepancies. The following chapter provides information on how demographic change can be counteracted. What are the negative associations of pensionable employees? Could the (continued) employment of older workers be an initial solution?

1.2 Current state of research

In order to understand the significance of these parties, it is important to know what an employee or employer actually is. According to the case law of the Federal Labour Court, an "employee is someone who, on the basis of a contract under private law, is obliged to perform work in the service of another person in personal dependence and bound by instructions .[7] On the other hand, only someone who has hired at least one other person as an employee within the framework of an employment relationship can be an employer. This employment relationship gives the employer the right to issue instructions, by virtue of which he can organise the specific performance obligation of

---

accessed on: 26/07/2017).

[3] Cf. Bpb (2012), http://www.bpb.de/nachschlagen/zahlen-und-fakten/soziale-situation-in- deutschland/147368/themengrafik-demografischer-wandel, (last accessed on: 26 July 2017).

[4] In the following, the term employer refers to both women and men.

[5] In the following, the term pensioners refers to both women and men.

[6] Cf. Wery (2015), p. 13 ff.

[7] Cf. judgement of the BAG of 9 March 2005, 5 AZR 493/04.

the employee in terms of type, place and time."[8] Employers can be natural persons, legal entities under private and public law[9] and commercial companies.[10] Currently, more and more employees of retirement age are becoming professionally active. According to the Generali Ageing Study, a full eleven per cent of these so-called "silver workers" are aged 65-86 and work around 15 hours a week. Before retirement, the figure is as high as twenty per cent, which means that one in five people aged 60-67 is in employment. [11] The Organisation for Economic Co-operation and Development (OECD) notes that the number of working people of German retirement age in Sweden is much higher, at eighty per cent. This is mainly due to the fact that the fixed retirement age has been abolished in Sweden. There, older employees are allowed to keep their jobs until at least the age of 67. Many pensioners often continue to work beyond this age.[12] According to the Federal Employment Agency, the number of employees aged 65 and over who are exclusively in marginal employment totalled 798,320 in December 2012, compared to 174,810 employees subject to social insurance contributions. It should be noted that people with an academic degree who are entitled to a pension are much more active in the labour market than people with lower qualifications, of whom only one in twenty is employed.

Conversely, this means that there are also different qualification levels among the so-called "silver workers".[13]

---

[8] Cf. Juraforum (n.d.), http://www.juraforum.de/lexikon/arbeitgeber, (last accessed on: 05/08/2017).

[9] GmbH, stock corporation, GbR, e.V.

[10] KG, oHG.

[11] Cf. Focus (2007), http://www.focus.de/finanzen/karriere/perspektiven/branchen/silver- workers_aid_131372.html, (last accessed on: 26 July 2017).

[12] Cf. Haas (2015), http://www.sueddeutsche.de/karriere/oecd-studie-zahl-der-arbeitnehmer-ueber-steigt-deutlich-1.1433767#redirectedFromLandingpage, (last accessed on: 26/07/2017).

[13] Cf. Deller (2013), Magazin der Bundesarbeitsgemeinschaft der Senioren-Organisationen, p.11, (last accessed on: 27.07.2017).

Chapter 2

2 Demographic change in Germany

Demography describes "the scientific study of the state of the population and its numerical changes (birth rate, immigration and emigration, age structure)". [14] As a result, change occurs when there is a change in the composition of a society, such as in the age structure or birth rate. The future deployment of pensioners is therefore dependent on demographic change. A change in demographics can mean both an increase and a decrease in the population. Three main factors play a role here: fertility, life expectancy and net migration. [15] Fertility represents the birth rate, which is measured by the fertility rate. Life expectancy describes the length of time a person is expected to live.[16] The last factor is net migration, which measures and integrates immigration to Germany in terms of numbers.

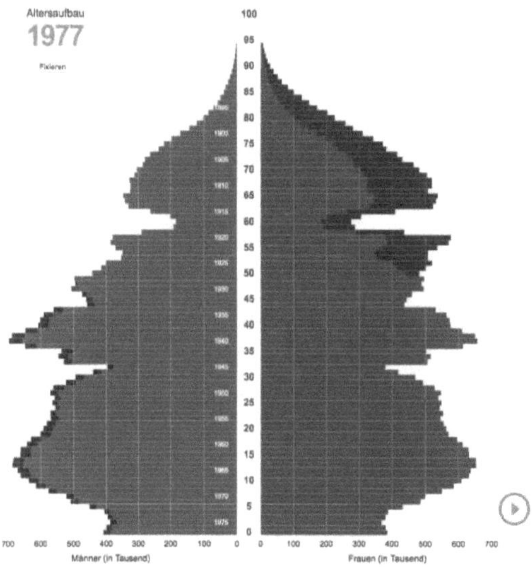

Figure 1: Population in Germany (1977)
Left (in thousands): Men/right (in thousands): Women

In this figure, which shows the demographic change in 1977, the different age groups are listed in

[14] Cf. cecu.de (n.d.), https://www.cecu.de/lexikon/politik/1747-demographie.htm, (last accessed on: 27/07/2017).

[15] Cf. Foerderland (n.d.), http://www.foerderland.de/mittelstand/demographischer-wandel/, (last accessed on: 27/07/2017).

[16] Cf. Duden (n.d.), http://www.duden.de/rechtschreibung/Lebenserwartung, (last accessed on: 27/07/2017).

relation to life expectancy. Accordingly, in 1977, 28 per cent of people were under the age of twenty. The twenty to 64 age group accounts for 57 per cent, while there are only 15 per cent of people over 65.[17]

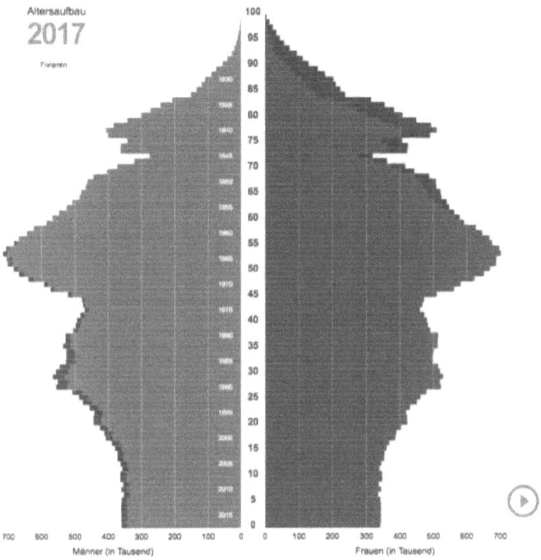

Figure 2: Coordinated population projection for Germany left (in thousands): Men/right (in thousands): Women

The next figure shows a statistical projection. In the current year 2017, the graph already shows an increase in life expectancy. This is also confirmed by the figures: The under-twenties make up 18 per cent of the population, the twenty to 64-year-olds make up sixty per cent and the over-65s now make up 22 18
per cent. The birth rate is expected to fall by ten per cent this year.[18]

[17] Cf. Federal Statistical Office (Destatis) (2015),https://service.destatis.de/bevoelkerungspyramide/#!y=2057&v=3, (last accessed on: 27 July 2017).

[18] Cf. Federal Statistical Office (Destatis) (2015),

https://service.destatis.de/bevoelkerungspyramide/#!y=2057&v=3, (last accessed on: 27.07.2017).

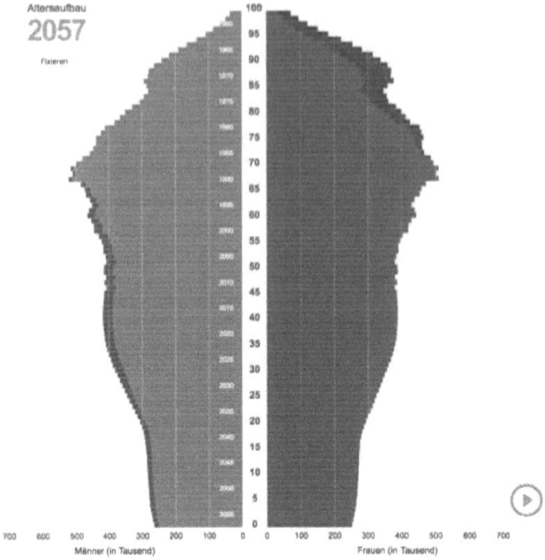

Figure 3: Coordinated population projection for Germany left (in thousands): Men/right (in thousands): Women

In the last figure, which shows a projection of forty years, the proportion of the youngest population group has fallen to 16 per cent. The group of twenty to 64-year-olds is also expected to decline to fifty per cent, while the group of senior citizens aged over 65 is expected to increase to 34 per cent.[19]

The drastic reduction in the birth rate combined with the increasing life expectancy will have a strong impact on the development of the German population in the long term. As the President of the Berlin-Brandenburg Academy of Sciences and Humanities (BBAW) Professor Günter Stock explains in an interview with "WeltN24", there are various reasons for demographic change and the decline in the birth rate. These could be , for example, reduced infant mortality, increasing sexual education or the sense of entitlement in society that family and career cannot be mastered together. [20]Furthermore, a steady "progress in medical care can be noted. According to health expert Dennis Haking, "hygiene, nutrition, housing, improved working conditions and material living standards" are reasons for an

[19] Cf. Federal Statistical Office (Destatis) (2015),

https://service.destatis.de/bevoelkerungspyramide/#!y=2057&v=3, (last accessed on: 27/07/2017).

[20] Cf. Lossau (2012), https://www.welt.de/wissenschaft/article109850347/Warum-die-Geburtenrate-in- Deutschland-niedrig-ist.html, (last accessed on: 28 July 2017).

expected increase in life expectancy.[21]

2.1 Impact on the potential labour force

The labour force potential is defined as the total of all employed and unemployed persons, including hidden reserves. In detail, this includes all people who are able to work, i.e. people of working age.[22]

Over the decades, there has been a downward trend in the number of people in employment. According to the Federal Statistical Office, the number of people in employment will fall significantly after 2020, reaching around forty million in 2035 and declining even further in 2060 until it finally reaches 36 million of working age.[23] Due to the upcoming retirement of the 1960s cohorts, the age structure will shift in favour of the middle age group (thirty to fifty years old) in the near future, while the number of people in employment will continue to fall. This means that companies will have a smaller and, above all, older labour force potential than today.[24]

---

[21] Cf. Haking (2017), p.11 f.

[22] Cf. Bpb (2013), https://www.bpb.de/nachschlagen/zahlen-und-fakten/soziale-situation-in- deutschland/61727/stille-reserve, (last accessed on: 29/07/2017).

[23] Cf. Federal Statistical Office (Destatis) (2009), https://www.destatis.de/DE/Publikationen/Thematisch/Bevoelkerung/VorausberechnungBevoelkerung/ BevoelkerungDeutschland2060Presse5124204099004.pdf?__blob=publicationFile, p. 7, (last accessed on: 29 July 2017).

[24] Cf. Federal Statistical Office (Destatis) (2009),

https://www.destatis.de/DE/Publikationen/Thematisch/Bevoelkerung/VorausberechnungBevoelkerung/Bevoelkerung Deutschland2060Presse5124204099004.pdf? ___blob=publicationFile, p.18, (last accessed on: 29/07/2017).

Chapter 3

3 The personnel bottleneck on the German labour market

Terms such as "staff shortages", "labour shortage", "skills shortage" or "skills gap" can often be found in various media. A fact that is now increasingly being discussed in society, in politics or in working life. Basically, all terms have one thing in common: the demand for labour is permanently higher than the supply of labour. This means that companies have more vacancies to fill than there are actually workers available. In practice, this can be, for example, few or no applications in response to a job advertisement. The labour force is defined as all persons capable of working, regardless of their qualifications[25].

Skilled workers form their own group independently of the labour force. Skilled workers are persons who have completed an academic education or recognised vocational training of at least two years. From a mathematical point of view, the available supply covers the overall economic demand, but there is still a shortage that needs to be counteracted. If this does not happen, there will be a shortage of skilled labour. At this point, the demand for skilled labour is no longer sufficiently covered over a longer period of time. There cannot be a shortage of skilled labour per se in the long term, as the employer would have to cover the demand in some other way, such as by extending working hours or using external labour. For this reason, the terms "staff shortage" or "skills gap" are more appropriate to describe this situation.[26]

Three groups can be potentially affected: The entire economy, certain regions or just certain occupational groups. Often only certain sectors or regions are affected.[27]

3.1 Possible causes of the labour shortage

As already described, demographic change is probably the biggest cause of staff shortages. The number of people in employment is continuing to fall, which can lead to a shortage of skilled labour . Another important aspect for many applicants is the location. Many people prefer to work in a large

---

[25] Cf. Kettner (2012), p. 15.

[26] Cf. Weise (2011), BWP vocational training in science and practice, p. 9f.

[27] Cf. Kettner (2012), p. 16.

city, as this is usually associated with a better range of jobs and technical progress. In rural areas, on the other hand, the situation is poorer. Employers find it more difficult to fill vacancies there, as "personal and professional prospects are usually rated lower in these regions".[28]

A final possible reason is the difference in qualification levels. The qualifications that jobseekers bring with them do not match the requirements of future employers. This is mainly due to the structural change in the economy. The service sector is becoming increasingly important, as is the new quaternary sector, the so-called "information and knowledge society". Older employees who have not had the opportunity to train in this area do not, in most cases, fulfil the requirements of younger, technically oriented companies. [29][30]

This results in what is known as a "mismatch". The following figure shows which qualities and characteristics are essential for most companies and employers.

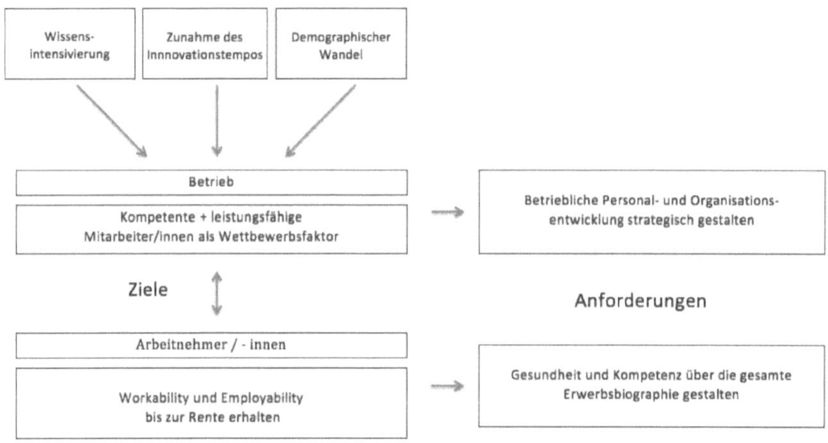

Figure 4: Requirements for companies and employees

(Source: Own illustration based on Prager/Schleiter) [30]

[28] Cf. Wery (2015), p. 13 ff.

[29] Cf. Wery (2015), p. 21.

[30] Cf. Prager / Schleiter (2010), p. 114.

3.2 Sectors most frequently affected by staff shortages

Although a labour shortage cannot be denied, according to the Federal Employment Agency it is "not universal". [31] According to this, "MINT professions" are particularly affected by staff shortages. These are professions related to maths, information technology, natural sciences and technology. The Federal Employment Agency has compiled statistics that summarise this fact in figures: Technical and health-related jobs in particular were vacant for longer periods of time. Care for the elderly and IT consulting are the "front runners". This is where the greatest demand exists.

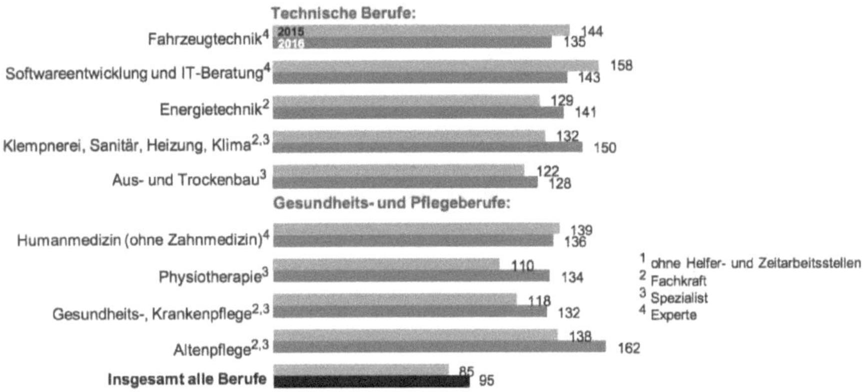

Figure 5: Average vacancy period for jobs subject to social security contributions in days of departure

Moving annual average, November to October in each case

(Source: Statistics from the Federal Employment Agency)

In most cases, the longer a position remains vacant, the greater the problems in finding a suitable candidate. In professions with a health and technical focus, the vacancy period[32] is the longest and it is therefore more difficult to find qualified candidates in these sectors. In comparison: The average vacancy period is ninety days.

3.3 Forecasts on the shortage of skilled labour (until 2030)

One way of preventing this is to draw up forecasts. These forecasts are intended to identify which

---

[31] Cf. PwC (2010), http://www.pwc.de/de/gesundheitswesen-und-pharma/assets/fachkraeftemangel.pdf, p.51, (last accessed on 30 July 2017).

[32] The period of time from the desired date of filling the position until it is vacated in days.

sectors or qualification groups could be affected by a supply surplus or a demand surplus in the future.

To this end, the Institute for Employment Research (IAB) and the Federal Institute for Vocational Education and Training (BIBB) have jointly prepared a forecast up to 2030 and divided it into two groups. On the one hand, the shortage of skilled labour is forecast by qualification level and, on the other, in specific occupations.[33]

Table 1: Forecasts of skills shortages by qualification level up to 2030

People without completed vocational training	People with completed vocational training	Master craftsmen, technicians, university
→Demand for labour is falling	→Supply decreasing due to demographic factors	→Supply and demand continue to rise
→Slow decline in supply	→Supply no longer meets demand	→For university graduates, demand is made up of replacement demand and new demand
→Slight increase in oversupply	→Shortage of skilled labour is increasing rapidly	→Replacement demand will increase significantly
→No better employment opportunities on the labour market in future	→Demand for qualified skilled labour will decline due to wage increases	→Academic oversupply is based on the current trend towards more academic degrees
→Early intervention / post-qualification programmes= Potential for mid-level skilled workers	→Supply≠ Specialist focus	→company demand increases

Source: Own illustration based on the BIBB Report 18/12

Table 2: Labour force by main occupational field, taking account of occupational migration up to 2030

Surplus demand until 2030	Surplus supply until 2030	Balanced situation until 2030
Machining, processing and repairing occupations	Machinery and equipment control and maintenance occupations	Occupations extracting raw materials
Trade and distribution occupations	Office and commercial service occupations	Traffic, storage, transport, security and guard occupations
Media, humanities and social sciences	Legal, management and economic professions	Technical and scientific professions
Health and social professions, body carers		Teaching professions
Artistic professions		

[33] Cf. bpb (2014), http://www.bpb.de/politik/innenpolitik/arbeitsmarktpolitik/178757/fachkraeftemangel?p=all, (last accessed on: 30/07/2017).

Catering and cleaning occupations		

Source: Own representation based on the BIBB Report 18/12

3.4 Different assessment of the staff shortage by SMEs and large companies

Two out of three small and medium-sized companies cannot find suitable employees or cannot fill their vacancies. This often leads to an impairment of competitiveness, especially if the competition finds the ideal employee [34] . The biggest problem for SMEs is the applicant's lack of professional qualifications or the labour supply, which is the cornerstone of a company's success.[35]

Although there is currently a tendency for the shortage of applicants to grow steadily, entrepreneurs are "much more optimistic today than they were a few years ago", according to the KfW Competence Centre for Research in Economy, Environment and Society. One third of SMEs considered hiring labour in 2010. In contrast, the figure has almost doubled within four years and now stands at sixty per cent. Another positive aspect is the fact that the labour market participation of women and older people has increased. In addition, immigrants from the EU are also significantly increasing the supply of skilled labour.[36]

However, this optimism will not last long, as it is likely that there will be demographically induced bottlenecks in the labour market in ten years' time. According to calculations by KfW, around 57 per cent of SMEs had problems recruiting suitable candidates in 2010. By comparison, in 2014 the figure was around 75 per cent Large companies have comparatively fewer recruitment problems than SMEs. Here too, the biggest problem is the search for employees with completed vocational training. Around 31 per cent of large companies have difficulties in their search. This figure rises to 46 per cent for SMEs, while small companies have the hardest time. Sixty per cent of small companies have problems finding candidates in this qualification group.

There are many reasons why large companies find it easier to find good quality candidates.

One important aspect concerns the lack of awareness or attractiveness of the respective company. Small and medium-sized companies are often associated with a lack of prospects and a lack of career

[34] In the following, the term "employee" refers to both women and men.

[35] Cf. Zeuner (n.d.), https://digitaler-mittelstand.de/business/ratgeber/fachkraeftemangel-koenigswege-aus-dem- personal-engpass-11502, (last accessed on: 30/07/2017).

[36] Cf. Leifels (2015), https://www.kfw.de/PDF/Download-Center/Konzernthemen/Research/PDF-Dokumente- Fokus-Volkswirtschaft/Fokus-Nr.-100-Juli-2015-Fachkr%C3%A4fterekrutierung-im-Mittelstand.pdf, (last accessed on: 01/08/2017).

and promotion opportunities. Furthermore, SMEs often have limited financial and time resources at their disposal, which means that there are fewer applicants for vacancies. The search for personnel often has to be cancelled. In many cases, vacancies are filled with applicants who are not a "perfect fit" for the qualifications and requirements. Another reason for the success of large corporations in the search for personnel is the fact that they have their own HR department, which focuses on finding potential candidates and also has the necessary expertise about the situation on the labour market.

In percentage terms, around 22 per cent of SMEs employ people who are specifically responsible for personnel management. On the other hand, 86 per cent of large corporations have their own HR department.[37]

---

[37] See Bußmann/ Seyda (2015),

https://www.kofa.de/fileadmin/Dateiliste/Publikationen/Studien/Fachkraefteengpaesse_in_Unternehmen_2015_Die Altersstruktur_in_Engpassberufen.pdf, p. 7f.

Chapter 4

4 Pensions

One possible source of potential candidates could be pensioners. As already mentioned, the birth rate has been falling steadily in recent years, while life expectancy is increasing at the same time. This is leading to a loss of balance, which is becoming a major challenge for the pension system. Triggered by a falling birth rate, young working people will no longer be able to finance pensioners.[38] Pensioners are employees who are no longer working due to old age or are no longer able to work.[39] The "pension" system is a complex construct that is entangled with many regulations. For example, not all age groups have the same standard retirement age. According to § 235 SGB VI paragraph 2, those born before 1947 may draw a pension from the age of 65. Furthermore, the retirement age for people born between 1947 and 1963 is gradually being raised. Finally, those born from 1964 onwards will only reach retirement age at 67.

Nevertheless, many politicians believe that the age should be raised even further. Former German President Joachim Gauck, for example, has criticised the current pension system. In his opinion, the statutory pension is far too focussed on defining an end, not a transition. Former German Chancellor Helmut Schmidt also expressed his opinion on this controversial topic: "If we want to maintain the welfare state, then we have to work longer. And in the distant future, we will have to work even longer than the age of 67". [40]

This was also the reason why former Labour Minister Franz Müntefering pushed through the retirement age of 67 in 2007.[41] It is becoming increasingly clear how serious the changes in the labour market triggered by demographic change are.

4.1 Advantages and opportunities, as well as disadvantages and risks

The employment of older workers has a number of advantages. On the one hand, older employees usually have many years of professional experience, for example knowledge of common production

---

[38] Cf. BMAS (2013), http://www.bmas.de/DE/Themen/Rente/was-ist-Rente.html, (last accessed on: 31/07/2017).

[39] Cf. wissen.de (n.d.), http://www.wissen.de/wortherkunft/rente, (last accessed on: 31/07/2017).

[40] Cf. Schwenn (2015), http://www.faz.net/aktuell/wirtschaft/rente-mit-63-sendet-falsche-signale-an-die-rentner-13547229.html, (last accessed on: 01/08/2017).

[41] Cf. Schwenn (2015), http://www.faz.net/aktuell/wirtschaft/rente-mit-63-sendet-falsche-signale-an-die-rentner-13547229.html, (last accessed on: 01/08/2017).

processes, how to operate equipment and how to deal with customers. Employers can utilise this knowledge and offer young employees in particular the opportunity to learn from older employees. [42]

On the other hand, employees over the age of fifty have familiarised themselves with corporate cultures and processes and can provide management with advice. Qualities such as punctuality, reliability, conscientiousness and a sense of responsibility are instilled and taught to every employee in the course of their career. Furthermore, older employees are usually in a different life situation than younger ones. Family planning is often already complete and career security is the top priority, which also minimises the risk of absences due to parental leave or pregnancy.[43]

Finally, the employee's burden in terms of unemployment and pension insurance is considerably reduced, as contributions are reduced with increasing age.[44]

Like many controversial topics, the continued employment of pensionable employees also has a downside. Although many years of professional experience are a valuable resource, they also have disadvantages. Under certain circumstances, it could prove difficult to replace methods and procedures that have already been learnt with new, innovative ideas. As a result, there is an increased risk that older employees will recognise the innovations and improvements or find it difficult to implement them in day-to-day operations. Another aspect that could speak against the reactivation of older employees is the acceptance of younger superiors or work colleagues. Workers of an advanced age often have experience that younger employees lack, whether professionally or personally. Professional or personal superiority could lead to a tense working atmosphere, as the values of the younger generation are not recognised. Simple standards or IT skills, which are now a prerequisite in every application process, make it difficult to consider older people who are willing to work but do not have such training. Another point is the scientifically proven decline in the ability to learn and absorb information with increasing age, as well as the steady decline in the ability to concentrate. Both the mental and physical development of each individual play a role in this and, together with the social environment, provide important support for the retention of older employees in the company. For this reason, the negative characteristics and associations can never be applied in full to all older employees. The problems listed are not only dependent on age itself, but on each person and

[42] Cf. Wery (2015), p.29.

[43] Cf. Wery (2015), p.29.

[44] Cf. Bäcker / Jansen / Schmitz (2017), p.21f.

their character. [45]

As employees get older, they increasingly suffer from health problems. This creates an unavoidable risk for the employer, which leads to disrupted processes within the company. In comparison, younger colleagues are sick much less often, but for longer.[46] Nowadays, companies are often on the lookout for people who are willing to work, who match the desired target group and who can identify with the corporate culture. Hiring an older employee can be both an advantage and a disadvantage. [47]

Dr Nicole Elert, Head of Employment Law at PricewaterhouseCoopers, emphasises how important it is to get rid of prejudices and stereotypes when it comes to older employees: "Despite the significantly higher esteem in which older employees are held today, there still seem to be stereotypes - for example that further training is no longer worthwhile for them or that employees of a certain age no longer want to develop. These misconceptions need to be dispelled, especially with regard to digitalisation."[48]

---

[45] Cf. Wery (2015), p.30.

[46] Cf. Wery (2015), p.31.

[47] Cf. Wery (2015), p.31.

[48] Cf. PwC (2017), http://www.pwc.de/de/pressemitteilungen/2017/vergleich-zu-oecd-deutschland-bei-integration- von-aelteren-arbeitnehmern-nur-mittelmass.html, (last accessed on: 02.08.2017).

Chapter 5

5 Measures to overcome demographic challenges by (further) employing retirees

Based on the staff shortage and the increasing lack of skilled labour, the state has endeavoured to develop an initial tangible approach that opens up new opportunities for both employers and retirees in terms of continued employment. In the following, one of these approaches is presented in the form of § 41 sentence 3 SGB VI, and a practical realisation of this legal text is explained in more detail.

5.1 Significance of § 41 SGB VI

Section 41 SGB VI was introduced in 1989 and regulates the employment relationship and protection against dismissal after reaching the standard retirement age. According to sentence 1, the "insured person's entitlement to an old-age pension is not to be regarded as a reason that may give rise to the termination of an employment relationship by the employer in accordance with the Dismissal Protection Act." This essentially means that the employment relationship is not automatically terminated once the employee reaches the standard retirement age or cannot be terminated for reasons of age.[49]

Sentence 2 also states: "An agreement that provides for the termination of an employee's employment relationship without notice at a time when the employee can apply for an old-age pension before reaching the standard retirement age is deemed to have been concluded with the employee upon reaching the standard retirement age, unless the agreement was concluded within the last three years prior to this time or was confirmed by the employee within the last three years prior to this time." This clause includes "that a possible early pension entitlement leads to the termination of the employment relationship if the employee has not agreed to this at an age close to retirement age".[50] According to the judgement of the Baden-Württemberg Higher Labour Court of 3 December 2014, this is intended to "protect the employee's power of disposition under social law", as the employee should have the opportunity to freely decide on the start of retirement before reaching the standard retirement age. Sentence 2 of Section 41 SGB VI is intended to ensure that a "possible early pension

---

[49] Cf. price (2015), p. 165.

[50] Cf. Deutscher Bundestag (2006), http://dipbtbundestag.de/dip21/btd/16/037/1603794.pdf#page=34, p.34, (last accessed on: 02/08/2017).

entitlement does not lead to the termination of the employment relationship".[51]

The important part of section 41 for many companies and employees is the newly added sentence 3, which offers both contracting parties new opportunities to postpone the existing employment relationship further. What this means for the parties in the narrower sense is explained in more detail below.

5.2 Scope of application of § 41 sentence 3 SGB VI

On 1 July 2014, the third sentence of Section 41 SGB VI was amended and came into force.

"The parties to the employment contract may postpone the date of termination by agreement during the employment relationship, if necessary several times, provided that an agreement provides for the termination of the employment relationship upon reaching the standard retirement age". Until this point in time, the restrictions of Section 14 TzBfG stood in the way of the conclusion of a further fixed-term employment contract.

According to Section 14 (1) TzBfG, "the limitation of an employment contract is permissible if it is justified by an objective reason. The first paragraph is risky in this respect, as an objective reason must be stated for each fixed-term contract in accordance with points 1 to 8. If an employee suspects that there is no objective reason or that it is not sufficient, they can take their employer to court in the course of an action for the cancellation of a fixed term in accordance with Section 17 TzBfG. If the objective reason does not stand up to judicial scrutiny in the further course, the employer must change the fixed-term contract to a "contract for an indefinite period" in accordance with Section 16 TzBfG. With Section 41 sentence 3 SGB VI, the legislator has closed the loophole that existed with Section 14 TzBfG and offered employers and employees the opportunity to implement fixed-term contracts at their own discretion. This provided a new resource for both sides.[52]

Prior to 1 July 2014, a fixed-term employment contract was only valid in accordance with Section 14 (3) sentence 1 TzBfG if the employee had reached the age of 52 and had been unemployed for at least four months within the meaning of Section 138 (1) sentence 1 SGB III immediately prior to the start of the fixed-term employment contract. In addition, according to Section 14 para. 3 sentence 2 TzBfG, a multiple extension of the employment relationship up to five years was possible. As a result of

---

[51] Cf. judgement of the LAG Baden-Württemberg of 03.12.2014, Ref. 4 Sa 48/14.

[52] Cf. Seel (2014), http://www.ddniedersachsen.de/uploads/media/Anlage_5______ Keine_Lust_auf_Ruhestand.pdf, p.1, (last accessed on 04/08/2017).

Section 14 TzBfG, the temporary direct continued employment of employees entitled to a pension was not possible in 2014. There were exceptions at the time in the course of case law. A subsequent fixed-term extension of a previously open-ended employment contract after reaching the standard retirement age was therefore effective in most cases. The basis for this decision was the objective reason pursuant to Section 14 (1) No. 6 TzBfG, according to which a fixed term is possible if "reasons relating to the person of the employee justify the fixed term".[53] In comparison, the new sentence 3 of Section 41 SGB VI represents a different regulation on the limitation of employment contracts. In this case, the lex specialis applies, according to which Section 41 sentence 3 SGB VI takes precedence over Section 14 (1) sentence 1 TzBfG.

It is important to note that certain conditions must be met for § 41 sentence 3 SGB VI to be effective and realised. Sentence 3 initially states: "If an agreement provides for the termination of the employment relationship upon reaching the standard retirement age [...]". A decisive prerequisite is therefore the existence of an agreement on the termination of the employment relationship upon reaching the standard retirement age. According to Section 35 SGB VI, this is generally reached at the age of 67. However, the gradual increase in the age limit must be taken into account here, as already explained in Chapter 4.

Sentence 3 also states: "[...] the parties to the employment contract may postpone the date of termination by agreement during the employment relationship, if necessary several times." Firstly, the retirement age must be precisely determined in order to establish when the "termination date" occurs. In addition, the agreement on a later termination date (the extension) must be concluded before the end of the employment relationship.

5.2.1 Individual agreements, collective agreements and legal fiction

When applying § 41 sentence 3 SGB VI, a distinction must be made between three essential "agreement types": The individual agreement, the collective agreement and the statutory fiction. "An individual agreement exists if both parties have expressly or tacitly negotiated an agreement. It is to be distinguished from general terms and conditions, where one party sets the conditions for the other."[54] Firstly, the written form requirement pursuant to Section 14 TzBfG is important, as the agreement is generally a significant component of the employment contract. Furthermore, according

---

[53] Cf. price (2015), p. 165.

[54] Cf. Friedrich-Schmid (2010), http://www.jura-basic.de/aufruf.php?file=7&art=6=&find=AGB_Vertragsklausel__Individualvereinbarung, (last accessed on: 04/08/2017).

to general principles, there must be a material reason for the validity of the fixed-term employment contract agreement. According to Section 14 (1) sentence 2 no. 6 TzBfG, a material reason is required in particular if "reasons relating to the employee justify the fixed term". These reasons could exist if the agreement is aligned with the statutory retirement pension and a link to the permanent receipt of a retirement pension is established. .[55]

On the other hand, there is the agreement in the collective agreement. This is a "form of contract that is not concluded between individual contracting parties, but is binding for a collective. The collective agreement also functions as a generic term for collective agreements and works agreements [...]".[56] According to the European Union's Equal Treatment Directive RL 2000/78/EC, the agreement in the collective agreement, which states that the employment relationship ends when the standard retirement age is reached, is effective without further requirements. The regulation is to be seen as positive in that both the employer and the employee gain stability through the foreseeable start of retirement.[57]

The third "agreement type" consists of the so-called "statutory fiction". According to the general definition, this refers to "the arrangement of the law to treat factual or legal circumstances as given, even though they do not actually exist. The fiction can establish the exact opposite of the actual circumstances as legally binding".[58] In addition to the express agreement to terminate the employment relationship, as in the case of an individual or collective agreement, an agreement within the meaning of Section 41 sentence 3 or, if applicable, Section 41 sentence 2 SGB VI is given by the fictional effect. This provision stipulates that an agreement "which provides for the termination of an employee's employment relationship without notice on the date on which the employee can apply for an old-age pension before reaching the standard retirement age is deemed to have been concluded with the employee on reaching the standard retirement age." The situation is different if the agreement was concluded within the last three years before this date or was confirmed by the employee within the last three years before this date. The "fictitious effect is to be qualified as an agreement within the

---

[55] See Preis (2015), p. 165.

[56] Cf. Krauth (n.d.), http://wirtschaftslexikon.gabler.de/Definition/kollektivvertrag.html, (last accessed on: 04/08/2017).

[57] Cf. Seel (2014), http://www.ddniedersachsen.de/uploads/media/Anlage_5______ Keine_Lust_auf_Ruhestand.pdf, p.3 (last accessed on: 04/08/2017).

[58] Cf. wissen.de (n.d.), http://www.wissen.de/lexikon/fiktion-recht (last accessed on: 04/08/2017).

meaning of sentence 3 in view of the regulatory purpose of § 41 SGB VI".[59]

According to § 41 sentence 3 SGB VI, the contracting parties can agree once or several times to postpone the termination date of the employment contract. This agreement is also to be regarded as a time limit. Unlike Section 14 (2) TzBfG, Section 41 sentence 3 SGB VI does not specify a maximum duration of the postponement. Furthermore, the number of permissible extensions is also missing. To summarise, Section 41 sentence 3 SGB VI is therefore less strictly regulated than Section 14 (2) TzBfG, whereby three extensions are possible up to a total duration of two years.

A further requirement is that the agreement on the "postponement" of the termination date must be formally concluded during the original employment relationship, i.e. no later than the last day of the month in which the standard retirement age is reached. It should also be noted that Section 41 sentence 3 does not regulate any later agreements. The new fixed-term contract must therefore be seamless, i.e. without

without interruption to the old employment relationship. Furthermore, no other changes may be made to the content, such as to working hours or similar. However, if the contracting parties wish to extend the contract under different conditions, this amended content must be inserted either before or after the extension is concluded, i.e. independently of the extension agreement. Otherwise, the new fixed term is invalid.[60]

5.3 Fixed-term employment contract

A fixed-term employment contract is a "contract that is concluded for a fixed term. The admissibility of fixed-term employment contracts is governed by the Part-Time and Fixed-Term Employment Act (TzBfG)"[61] .

---

[59] Cf. Seel (2014), http://www.ddniedersachsen.de/uploads/media/Anlage_5______ Keine_Lust_auf_Ruhestand.pdf, p. 3, (last accessed on: 04/08/2017).

[60] Cf. Seel (2014), http://www.ddniedersachsen.de/uploads/media/Anlage_5______ Keine_Lust_auf_Ruhestand.pdf, p. 4, (last accessed on: 04/08/2017).

[61] Cf. Wichert (n.d.), http://wirtschaftslexikon.gabler.de/Definition/befristeter-arbeitsvertrag.html, (last accessed on: 04/08/2017).

As soon as an employee is about to reach retirement age, they have the option of continuing their employment relationship for a fixed term. This does not constitute discrimination against the employee on the grounds of age within the meaning of Section 10 sentence 3 no. 5 AGG in conjunction with EU Directive 2000/78/EC, as no less favourable treatment compared to other employees is discernible. According to Section 10 sentence 3 no. 5 AGG, there is no discrimination in the case of an "agreement that provides for the termination of the employment relationship without notice at a time when the employee can apply for an old-age pension". According to the ECJ, retirement age clauses in collective labour agreements and employment contracts are objectively justified and permissible under European law. The justification can generally be found in the factual reasons in Section 14 (1) TzBfG. These contain reasons for a fixed term or a fixed term for a specific purpose. The BAG's decision of 11 February 2015 shows that reaching the statutory retirement age or receiving a pension is not a legitimate objective reason under Section 14 (1) TzBfG.[62] The employment contract of the 65-year-old plaintiff did not contain a clause that provided for the termination of the employment relationship upon reaching the standard retirement age. His employment contract was extended twice for a limited period after he reached retirement age. His contract was then due to end on 31 December 2011, as he was supposed to have trained his successor by this date. - The action for cancellation of the fixed term followed after the plaintiff wanted to continue his employment contract for a fixed term for the third time, but the defendant refused. The defendant argued that the substantive reason pursuant to Section 14 (1) No. 6 TzBfG was legal in this case, which the BAG rejected. According to the BAG, the entitlement to a pension and the receipt of a pension are neither proper as a substantive reason nor as a reason for a subsequent fixed-term employment contract.[63] It is necessary for the fixed term to "serve the defendant's concrete plans for the next generation". The employer must treat the employee in the same way as any other of its employees.

Although Section 41 sentence 3 SGB VI offers companies and their employees entitled to a pension the option of continuing the employment relationship for a fixed term even without a material reason, this provision is only relevant in accordance with the first half of the sentence if the employment contract already contains a retirement age clause. In the present case, this is not the case, meaning that there is no interference. The BAG ruled in favour of the plaintiff and against the defendant. Accordingly, the employer is not authorised to enter into fixed-term agreements with the employee

[62] Cf. judgement of the BAG of 11/02/2015, 7 AZR 17/13

[63] Cf. Hensche (2015), https://www.hensche.de/Befristete_Beschaeftigung_im_Rentenalter_BAG_7AZR17-13_11.02.2015_13.51.html, (last accessed on: 05.08.2017).

entitled to a pension that deprive the employee of legal protection.[64]

As an interim result, it should be noted that the continued employment of retirees in accordance with the rules of Section 14 (1) TzBfG and Section 41 sentence 3 SGB VI is a suitable means for employers to close bottlenecks, as the company continues to employ candidates who are well trained and already familiar with the operational processes.[65] From a legal perspective, however, there are a few rules to bear in mind. "Those who reach retirement age do not automatically leave the employment relationship, but rather only if a retirement age clause provides for this. If neither a retirement age clause under labour law nor a collective agreement applies to the employment relationship, the employment relationship continues to exist despite the pension entitlement and can then be terminated by a termination agreement or limited in time by a fixed-term agreement".[66]

---

64 Cf. Hensche (2015), https://www.hensche.de/Befristete_Beschaeftigung_im_Rentenalter_BAG_7AZR17-13_11.02.2015_13.51.html, (last accessed on: 05/08/2017).

[65] Cf. Gloistein & Partner (n.d.), http://www.gloistein-partner.de/arbeitsverhaeltnis-mit-rentnern-was-ist-bei-der-beschaeftigung-altersrentnern-zu-beachten, (last accessed on: 05/08/2017).

[66] Cf. Hensche (2015), https://www.hensche.de/Befristete_Beschaeftigung_im_Rentenalter_BAG_7AZR17-13_11.02.2015_13.51.html, (last accessed on: 05/08/2017).

Chapter 6

6 Case study Bremen Regional Labour Court 3 Sa 78/16 3

The new Section 41 sentence 3 SGB VI does not initially appear to have any gaps or difficulties and should be viewed favourably, especially for pensioners. The following legal dispute shows that the new provision is not entirely without gaps. In the second instance, the employer and employee are in dispute about the limitation of the employment relationship and the entitlement to the default of acceptance wage after termination of the employment contract.

6.1 Facts of the case

The plaintiff, who worked as a teacher at a state school, would have to leave the teaching profession on 31 January 2015 due to his age in accordance with Section 44 TV-L Special regulations for employees as teachers No. 4 to Section V Fixed-term employment and termination of employment. In a letter dated February, the plaintiff applied for continued employment beyond the standard retirement age until the end of the 2015/16 school year.
In October 2014, both parties reach the following agreement:

"Between ..., represented by ... and Mr H. J. born on ...1949, the following agreement is concluded in accordance with Section 41 sentence 3 SGB VI in conjunction with Section 30 (1) sentence 1 TV-L: The automatic termination of the employment relationship [...] pursuant to § 44 No. 4 TV-L is postponed until 31 July 2015. The employment relationship shall end at the end of this date without the need for notice of termination. [...]".

Before 31 July 2015, the plaintiff submitted a further application for continued employment until the end of the 2015/2016 school term. In a notification dated May 2015, the school administration rejected this application. He then filed an action against his employer for review of the fixed-term contract and also demanded payment of the salary for default of acceptance for the period after his dismissal.[67]

[67] Cf. Hensche (2017), https://www.hensche.de/Hinausschieben-der-Altersgrenze-unbegrenzte-Befristungsmoeglichkeit-LAG-Bremen-3Sa78-16-29.05.2017.html, (last accessed on: 05/08/2017).

6.2 Judgement

As this case concerns issues relating to European law, the legal dispute was initially suspended by the Bremen Higher Labour Court and referred to the European Court of Justice with unanswered questions. One question that the Bremen Higher Labour Court was unable to answer or on which no agreement was reached concerned Section 5 of the framework agreement on fixed-term employment contracts. This calls on the member states to draw up preventative regulations with regard to the so-called "chain limitation" in order to prevent the abuse of fixed-term employment contracts.
These must include the following: "[...] objective reasons justifying the renewal of such contracts or relationships; the maximum total authorised duration of successive employment contracts or relationships and the authorised number of renewals of such contracts or relationships". As described in Chapter 5.2, the legislator has already taken an important step towards realising the EU-compliant requirements with Section 14 TzBfG by specifying the objective reasons that justify a further fixed term in Paragraph 1 and the maximum permissible duration in Paragraph 3. However, with Section 41 Sentence 3 SGB VI, the legislator has given companies and employees entitled to a pension the option of continuing the employment relationship as often as they wish, even after retirement age, without more precise delimitations or restrictions on the possibility of a fixed term.

For this reason, the ECJ will first examine the extent to which Section 5 of the EU Directive and the newly amended third sentence of Section 41 SGB VI are compatible with each other. Furthermore, the question remains as to whether this constitutes age discrimination, as Section 41 sentence 3 SGB VI stipulates that only employees entitled to a pension have the option of continuing their fixed-term employment relationship frequently, while this is not permitted for younger employees. Overall, Section 41 sentence 3 SGB VI still has some legal loopholes that the ECJ must now clarify.[68]

6.3 Problem definition of § 41 sentence 3 SGB VI

The discussion about § 41 sentence 3 SGB VI must be settled by the ECJ. The LAG Bremen refers to the fact that § 41 sentence 3 and Article 5 no. 1 of the framework agreement on fixed-term employment contracts contradict each other, as there are no grounds for justification. According to the LAG Bremen, facilitating the induction of subsequent employees is not a legitimate reason, as the employer is aware of the employee's age and could have taken care of the induction of the new

[68] Cf. Hensche (2017), https://www.hensche.de/Hinausschieben-der-Altersgrenze-unbegrenzte- Befristungsmoeglichkeit-LAG-Bremen-3Sa78-16-29.05.2017.html, (last accessed on: 05/08/2017).

employee early enough.

Overall, Section 41 sentence 3 SGB VI leaves many questions unanswered, such as whether this provision is dispositive of collective agreements. It is also not clear whether it only regulates an extension of the employment relationship or whether it also includes changes to the content of the employment contract. A fundamental problem is the question of where the maximum limit lies. Has the legislator achieved its goal with the new regulation of § 41 sentence 3 SGB VI? Could employment contracts concluded with employees entitled to a pension be extended as often as desired? There are doubts about this. There are sufficient reasons to assume that Section 41 sentence 3 SGB VI violates European law, for example Article 6 of Directive 2000/78/EC. According to this, "differences of treatment on grounds of age shall not constitute discrimination if they are objective, proportionate [...] and justified by a legitimate aim [...]".[69]
Furthermore, Art. 6 of Directive 2000/78/EC explains three scenarios of justified unequal treatment. Scenario a) of Art. 6 is generally used as the most common justification. While scenarios b) and c) regard the setting of a minimum or maximum age as justifiable under certain conditions, scenario a) regards a measure to pursue a specific objective as legitimate. Accordingly, "such unequal treatment may include, in particular: (a) the establishment of special conditions of access to employment and vocational training and special conditions of employment and working conditions, including conditions of dismissal and remuneration, in order to promote the integration into employment of young people, older workers and persons with caring responsibilities or to ensure their protection."[70] This means that the continued limitation of the employment contract is justified for the integration or familiarisation of a new employee. The new regulation according to sentence 3 of Section 41 SGB VI implicitly allows contracts with employees entitled to a pension to be continued for an unlimited period of time without any restriction or maximum limit. In addition, the fixed-term contracts must comply with the fixed-term directive of § 5 of Directive 1999/70/EC. Section 41 sentence 3 SGB VI does not specify a permissible duration for the fixed-term employment contract within the meaning of Section 5 no. 1b of the Directive, nor does it specify the number of times the contract may be continued for a fixed term in accordance with Section 5 no. 1c. Companies should be aware that there are many risks associated with the use of this new provision. For them and also for employees entitled to a pension, §41 sentence 3 SGB VI opens up new possibilities for the desired continued employment, but is ultimately not as secure as the fixed term in accordance with

[69] Cf. Art. 6 of Directive 2000/78/EC (2000).

[70] Cf. Art. 6 of Directive 2000/78/EC (2000).

§ 14 TzBfG with the use of the aforementioned objective reasons. At this point, the legislator must ensure that the new regulations are in line with European law, as there is a gap in the law. A possible solution to this loophole is presented below.

6.4 Draft contract

Extension of the employment contract beyond the standard retirement age (sample)

The sample[71] contains the following wording for the **first extension**:

1. employer and employee agree to postpone the automatic termination of the employment relationship due to reaching the standard retirement age in accordance with Section 41 sentence 3 SGB VI until *[date]*. The employment relationship shall end at the end of the aforementioned period without the need for notice of termination.

The following wording exists for a **further extension agreement:**

The employer and employee agree that the employment relationship existing between them will not end upon reaching the retirement date specified in the extension agreement pursuant to Section 41 sentence 3 SGB VI of *[date]*, but will continue until *[date]*.
The fixed term is based on the following objective reason in accordance with Section 14 TzBfG:[72]

- *Due to the temporary operational need for the project [...]*
- *Following the previous employment relationship.*
- *To replace Mrs/Mr .... for the duration of her/his illness/parental leave.*

parental leave.

- *For the purpose of trialling (max. 6 months)[.]*
- *At the employee's own request, as[.]*

[71] The model is based on Section 41 sentence 3 SGB VI and Section 14 (1) sentence 2 TzBfG.

[72] As Section 41 sentence 3 SGB VI does not specify adequate objective reasons or maximum limits with regard to further fixed-term contracts, the objective reasons of Section 14 (1) sentence 2 TzBfG are adopted here in a modified form.

The employment relationship ends at the end of *[date]* without the need for notice of termination.

2. unconditional fixed-term employment is possible *a maximum of five times* within *five years*, **taking into account the objective reasons** pursuant to Section 14 (1) sentence 2 TzBfG. A fixed term **without a material reason** is possible *three times within five years*.[73]

3. in all other respects, the previous agreements between the parties, in particular on the basis of the employment contract dated ________________ *[date]*, last amended on ___________ *[date]* shall remain unchanged.[74]

____

Place/date/signature of employee

____

Place/date/signature of employer

[73] The use of a maximum limit, taking into account the objective reasons, was added in line with Section 14 (2) and (3) TzBfG.

[74] It is assumed that neither collective agreements nor works agreements are used.

Chapter 7

7 Possible solutions on the part of companies

The draft agreement presented in Chapter 6.4 offers the legislator the opportunity to fill the legal loophole created by Section 41 sentence 3 SGB VI. It is essential that additional conditions and restrictions be included in this provision in the long term.

However, solutions do not necessarily have to come from the legislator. In their freedom of contract under Article 2 (1) of the German Constitution and Section 311 (1) of the German Civil Code (BGB), companies also have the opportunity to find their own way to cover their shortage of skilled labour by employing retirees. What companies can actually do and what is already practised in many companies is explained in more detail below.

One way to (continue to) employ retirees is through freelance work on a self-employed basis. According to § 18 EStG, freelance work includes in particular the self-employed medical professions, legal, tax and business advisory professions, scientific/technical professions and information-providing professions/cultural professions.
If the employee works in a managerial capacity, freelance work is also possible in accordance with § 18 sentence 2 EStG. The basic prerequisite for this is that the person "acts in a managerial capacity and on their own responsibility on the basis of their own expertise" in accordance with Section 18 sentence 3 EStG.
Freelance work has a number of advantages over business registration. No business has to be registered and no compulsory IHK membership is required. Furthermore, registration in the commercial register is not necessary and VAT does not have to be paid until the money is received.[75]
Freelancers have the opportunity to work in a company on a project basis for a certain period of time. These so-called project contracts can be extended as often as required or, if necessary, reissued.

An alternative is flexitime work. This is another option for employees entitled to a pension to adapt their working conditions to their wishes. The simplest type of flexitime work is to freely organise the start and end times of work within a flexitime period defined by . Another type is so-called qualified

[75] Cf. Arbeitsratgeber (2015), http://www.arbeitsratgeber.com/freiberuflich-arbeiten/, (last accessed on: 06.08.2017).

flexitime. The employee is free to decide on the duration of working hours on their working days. Plus or minus hours are also an option here, but these must be compensated for. This is an alternative to the fixed-term contract described above, as the pensioner has better time management and better control over private and business matters. Employees can benefit more from the personal adjustment of working hours, as they are given the opportunity to adapt their lives to their working day and vice versa.[76]

Another option is part-time work for older employees. This involves reducing working hours to a level below full-time employment. Legislation originally provided for a reduction in the working hours of a previously full-time employee entitled to a pension from, for example, forty to twenty hours during the last few years before retirement.[77] The block model is a method that is very popular in practice: here, the partial retirement phase is divided into two periods: the working phase and the release phase.
During the working phase, the employee continues to work as usual to the same extent as before and then stops working at all during the release phase. In both models, both remuneration and working hours are reduced over the entire period of partial retirement.[78]

Section 1 AltTZG refers to the aim of partial retirement. It states: "Partial retirement is intended to enable older employees to make a smooth transition from working life to retirement." Both employees and employers can benefit from partial retirement. A gradual reduction in working hours makes it easier to transfer knowledge from the future pensioner to the new employee, new jobs are created for younger employees and the employee is generally more satisfied due to the reduced workload. Employees are offered a smooth transition into retirement and the opportunity to pass on the knowledge they have acquired. In addition, earlier retirement and greater satisfaction result in a higher quality of life in old age.
There is also a downside to this type of employment. Under certain circumstances, part-time work could lead to organisational difficulties on the part of the employer, as slow processes can be expected due to the reduced working hours. Additional financial expenditure cannot be ruled out either. The

---

[76] Cf. Back (n.d.), http://www.arbeitszeit-klug-gestalten.de/alles-zu-arbeitszeitgestaltung/arbeitszeitmodelle-im-ueberblick/gleitzeit/, (last accessed on: 06/08/2017).

[77] This model is also known as the continuity or reduction model.

[78] Cf. Hensche (2017), https://www.hensche.de/Rechtsanwalt_Arbeitsrecht_Handbuch_Altersteilzeit.html, (last accessed on: 06/08/2017).

employee earns a significantly lower income with this method than with full-time work, which is consequently associated with lower pension payments.

Chapter 8

8 Conclusion

The personnel shortage or shortage of skilled labour has not been an unknown problem in Germany for a long time. For years, large, small and medium-sized companies have been struggling with the increasing shortage.

As already stated in this paper, this bottleneck is primarily the result of steadily increasing life expectancy, while the birth rate continues to fall. There is a decline in the younger generation, which means that there will be significantly more older workers over the years. This shortage is most pronounced in the STEM professions[79] . At this point, an attempt should be made not to view older workers who are about to retire as a disadvantage and a burden, but rather as a valuable resource to counteract the shortage of skilled labour. As a result, there is an option to (continue to) employ employees who are eligible for retirement. With Section 14 TzBfG and the new regulation of Section 41 sentence 3 SGB VI, the legislator has made an attempt and taken a step in the right direction.

Retired or working employees who are about to retire are thus given the option of continuing their employment relationship for a limited period.

However, as the case of the Bremen Higher Labour Court has shown, in which an employee successfully enforced an action for control of fixed-term employment on the basis of Section 41 sentence 3 SGB VI, the new provision is still incomplete and also does not comply with European law. It is the duty of the legislator to fill this gap in the law immediately. Compatibility with Section 5 of the framework agreement on fixed-term employment contracts must be a prerequisite here.

Companies are advised to use Section 14 TzBfG for fixed-term agreements with pensioners for the time being, as it is nowhere near as risky as Section 41 sentence 3 SGB VI. In addition, the draft contract template in Chapter 6.4 also offers an alternative solution, as this draft contains the important and legally legitimate elements from both laws and still allows both sides room for negotiation.
Finally, on the company side, the already familiar methods of continued employment should also be

[79] Occupations with a focus on maths, information technology, science and technology.

used, such as freelance work or flexitime or part-time work for older employees. This also offers employers a secure way of covering staff shortages in the long term.

In conclusion, it should be noted that the law as a whole is still immature and too utopian in its expectations. Following the criticism from the legal and company-related side, it remains to be seen whether the legislator will eliminate the points of criticism in the near future.

Bibliography

Labour Guide (2015): *Freelance professions or freelance work*
Available at: http://www.arbeitsratgeber.com/freiberuflich-arbeiten/ (last accessed on: 06/08/2017)

Back, Simone (n.d.): *Flexitime*
Available at: http://www.arbeitszeit-klug-gestalten.de/alles-zu-arbeitszeitgestaltung/arbeitszeitmodelle-im-ueberblick/gleitzeit/ (last accessed on: 06/08/2017)

Bäcker, Gerhard/ Jansen, Andreas /Schmitz, Jutta (2017): *Retirement only from 70? Problems and perspectives of the age transition*, Duisburg, IAQ-Forschung

Bpb (2014) : *Skilled labour shortage*
Available at:
http://www.bpb.de/politik/innenpolitik/arbeitsmarktpolitik/178757/fachkraeftemangel?p=all (last accessed on: 30.07.2017)

Bpb (2012) : *Facts and figures, the social situation in Germany-Demographic change*
Available at: http://www.bpb.de/nachschlagen/zahlen-und-fakten/soziale-situation-in-deutschland/147368/themengrafik-demografischer-wandel, (last accessed on: 26.07.2017)

Bpb (2012) : *Facts and figures, the social situation in Germany-Stille Reserve*
Available at: https://www.bpb.de/nachschlagen/zahlen-und-fakten/soziale-situation-in-deutschland/61727/stille-reserve
(last accessed on: 29/07/2017)

Federal Labour Court (2015): *Judgement of 11.02.2015,-7 AZR 17/13*
Available at: http://juris.bundesarbeitsgericht.de/cgi-bin/rechtsprechung/document.py?Gericht=bag&Art=en&nr=18106
(last accessed on: 05/08/2017)

Federal Labour Court (2005): *Judgement of 9 March 2005, -5 AZR 493/04*
Available at: http://lexetius.com/2005,789
(last accessed on: 05/08/2017)

Federal Ministry of Labour and Social Affairs (2013): *What is a pension?*
Available at: http://www.bmas.de/DE/Themen/Rente/was-ist-Rente.html
(last accessed on: 31/07/2017)

Bußmann, Sebastian / Seyda, Susanne (2015): *The age structure in bottleneck occupations*
Available at:
https://www.kofa.de/fileadmin/Dateiliste/Publikationen/Studien/Fachkraefteengpaesse_in_Untern
ehmen_2015_Die_Altersstruktur_in_Engpassberufen.pdf
(last accessed on: 31/07/2017)

Federal Statistical Office (2015): *13th Coordinated Population Projection for Germany*
Available at: https://service.destatis.de/bevoelkerungspyramide/#!y=2057&v=3 (last accessed on: 27/07/2017)

Federal Statistical Office (2009): *12th Coordinated Population Projection for Germany*
Available at:
https://www.destatis.de/DE/Publikationen/Thematisch/Bevoelkerung/VorausberechnungBevoelk
erung/BevoelkerungDeutschland2060Presse5124204099004.pdf?__blob=publicationFile (last accessed on: 29/07/2017)

Deller , Jürgen (2013): *The magazine of the Federal Working Group of Senior Citizens' Organisations*
Available at: http://www.bagso.de/fileadmin/Aktuell/BN/2013/BAGSO-
Nachrichten_4_2013.pdf
(last accessed on: 27.07.2017)

German Bundestag (2006): *Draft law of the CDU/CSU and SPD parliamentary groups Draft law to adjust the standard retirement age to demographic developments and to strengthen the financial basis of the statutory pension insurance scheme (RV-*
Age Limit Adjustment Act)
Available at: http://dipbt.bundestag.de/dip21/btd/16/037/1603794.pdf#page=34
(last accessed on: 02/08/2017)

Duden (n.d.): *Definition of life expectancy*

Available at: http://www.duden.de/rechtschreibung/Lebenserwartung
(last accessed on: 27/07/2017)

FOCUS Online (2007): *60 is far from the end*
http://www.focus.de/finanzen/karriere/perspektiven/branchen/silver-workers_aid_131372.html (last accessed on: 26/07/2017)

Förderland (undated): *The demographic development as a challenge*
Available at: http://www.foerderland.de/mittelstand/demographischer-wandel
(last accessed on: 27.07.2017)

Friedrich-Schmid, Volker (2010): *Individual agreement*
Available at: http://www.jura-basic.de/aufruf.php?file=7&art=6=&find=AGB_Vertragsklausel__Individualvereinbarung (last accessed on: 04.08.2017)

Legal fiction (n.d.)
Available at: http://www.wissen.de/lexikon/fiktion-recht (last accessed on: 04/08/2017)

Gloistein & Partner (n.d.): *Employment relationship with pensioners - What should be considered when employing old-age pensioners?*
Available at: http://www.gloistein-partner.de/arbeitsverhaeltnis-mit-rentnern-was-ist-bei-der-beschaeftigung-altersrentnern-zu-beachten
(last accessed on: 05/08/2017)

Haas, Sibylle (2012): *OECD study-Number of workers over 60 increases significantly*
Available at: http://www.sueddeutsche.de/karriere/oecd-studie-zahl-der-arbeitnehmer-ueber-increases-significantly-1.1433767#redirectedFromLandingpage
(last accessed on: 26/07/2017)

Haking, Dennis (2017): *Hygiene Management and Infection Prevention*, Berlin, LIT Verlag Dr. W. Hopf

Hensche, Martin (2017): *Partial retirement*
Available at:

https://www.hensche.de/Rechtsanwalt_Arbeitsrecht_Handbuch_Altersteilzeit.html
(last accessed on: 06/08/2017)

Hensche, Martin (2017): *Postponement of the retirement age in accordance with Section 41 sentence 3 SGB VI*
Available at: https://www.hensche.de/Hinausschieben-der-Altersgrenze-unbegrenzte-Befristungsmoeglichkeit-LAG-Bremen-3Sa78-16-29.05.2017.html
(last accessed on: 05/08/2017)

Hensche, Martin (2015): *Temporary employment at retirement age*
Available at:
https://www.hensche.de/Befristete_Beschaeftigung_im_Rentenalter_BAG_7AZR17-13_11.02.2015_13.51.html
(last accessed on: 05/08/2017)

Juraforum (n.d.): *Employers*
Available at: http://www.juraforum.de/lexikon/arbeitgeber
(last accessed on: 05/08/2017)

Kettner, Anja (2012): *Skilled labour shortage - fact or fiction?*, Bielefeld: W. Bertelsmann Verlag GmbH & Co KG,

Krauth, Christian (n.d.): *Collective agreement*
Available at: http://wirtschaftslexikon.gabler.de/Definition/kollektiwertrag.html
(last accessed on: 04/08/2017)

Baden-Württemberg Regional Labour Court (2014): *Judgement of 3 December·2014 - Ref. 4 Sa 48/14*
Available at: https://openjur.de/u/754676.html
(last accessed on 03/08/2017)

Leifels, Arne (2015): *Recruiting skilled labour in SMEs: Optimism must not obscure the not obscure qualification problems*
Available at: https://www.kfw.de/PDF/Download-Center/Konzernthemen/Research/PDF-Documents-Fokus-Volkswirtschaft/Fokus-No.-100-Juli-2015-Fachkr%C3%A4fterekrutierung- im-

Mittelstand.pdf
(last accessed on: 01/08/2017)

Lossau, Nobert (2012): *Why the birth rate in Germany is low*
Available at: https://www.welt.de/wissenschaft/article109850347/Warum-die-Geburtenrate-in-Deutschland-niedrig-ist.html (last accessed on 28/07/2012)

Portal for Finance and Insurance (n.d.): *Demography*
Available at: https://www.cecu.de/lexikon/politik/1747-demographie.htm (last accessed on: 27.07.2017)

Prager, Jens / Schleiter, Andre (2010): *Living, working and getting involved for longer,* Gütersloh: Verlag Bertelsmann Stiftung

Preis, Ulrich (2015): *Der Arbeitsvertrag Handbuch der Vertragsgestaltung*, 5th edition, Ottoschmidt Verlag

Press and Information Office of the Federal Government (2017)
Available at:
https://www.bundesregierung.de/ContentArchiv/DE/Archiv17/Interview/2013/08/2013-08-08-merkel-ula.html
(last accessed on: 26/07/2017)

PWC (2017): *Germany only mediocre at integrating older workers*
Available at: http://www.pwc.de/de/pressemitteilungen/2017/vergleich-zu-oecd-deutschland-in-integration-of-older-workers-only-mediocre.html
(last accessed on: 02/08/2017)

PWC (2010): *Skilled labour shortage*
Available at: http://www.pwc.de/de/gesundheitswesen-und-pharma/assets/fachkraeftemangel.pdf
(last accessed on: 30/07/2017)

Pension dictionary of origin (n.d.)
Available at: http://www.wissen.de/wortherkunft/rente

(last accessed on: 31/07/2017)

Swedish screenwriter (1918 - 2007): *The Art of Ageing*
Available at: http://www.kunst-des-alterns.de/zitate/
(last accessed on: 06/06/2017)

Schwenn, Kerstin (2015): *Live longer, work longer*
Available at: http://www.faz.net/aktuell/wirtschaft/rente-mit-63-sendet-falsche-signale-an-die-rentner-13547229.html
(last accessed on: 01/08/2017)

Seel, Henning-Alexander (2014): *No desire to retire - temporary (continued) work according to the new legal situation*
Available at:
http://www.ddniedersachsen.de/uploads/media/Anlage_5__Keine_Lust_auf_Ruhestand.pdf (last accessed on: 04/08/2017)

Weise, Frank-Jürgen (2011): *BWP-Berufsbildung in Wissenschaft und Praxis*, Issue 03/2011, W.Bertelsmann publishing house

Wery, Sarah (2015): *50plus in Zeiten des Fachkräftemangels,* 1st edition, Marburg: Tectum Marburg publishing house

Wichert, Joachim (n.d.): *fixed-term employment contract*
Available at: http://wirtschaftslexikon.gabler.de/Definition/befristeter-arbeitsvertrag.html (last accessed on: 04/08/2017)

Zeuner, Jörg (2014): *Staff shortages: The ideal way out of the bottleneck*
Available at: digitaler mittelstand, https://digitaler-mittelstand.de/business/ratgeber/fachkraeftemangel-koenigswege-aus-dem-personal-engpass-11502
(last accessed on: 30/07/2017)

Appendix

Bremen Regional Labour Court

3 Sa 78/16 3

Ca 3165/15

DESCRIPTION

In the legal dispute

Plaintiff and appellant, Proz.-Bev:

against

Defendant and appellant, Proz.-Bev:

the 3rd Chamber of the Bremen Regional Labour Court, on the basis of the hearing on 23 November 2016, by

the presiding judge at the Regional Labour Court the honorary judge

the honorary judge

recognised the law:

1. the following questions are referred to the Court of Justice of the European Union pursuant to Article 267 of the Treaty on the Functioning of the European Union (TFEU):

Is Clause 5(1) of the Framework Agreement on fixed-term work concluded on 18 March 1999, annexed to Council Directive 1999/70/EC of 28 June 1999 concerning the framework agreement on fixed-term work concluded by ETUC, UNICE and CEEP, to be interpreted as precluding national legislation which allows the parties to an employment contract, without further conditions, to terminate the agreed employment relationship on reaching the standard length of service without any time limit?

the agreed termination of the employment relationship on reaching the standard retirement age by agreement during the employment relationship, possibly several times, merely because the employee is entitled to an old-age pension on reaching the standard retirement age?

2. if the Court answers question 1 in the affirmative:

Does the incompatibility of the national provision referred to in Question 1 with Article 5(1) of the Framework Agreement also apply in the case of the first postponement of termination?

(3) Are Article 1, Article 2(1) and Article 6(1) of Council Directive 2000/78/EC of 27 November 2000 establishing a general framework for the protection of employees? Are Articles 1, 2(1) and 6(1) of Council Directive 2000/78/EC of 27 November 2000 establishing a general framework for equal treatment in employment and occupation (Directive 2000/78/EC) and/or the general principles of Community law to be interpreted as precluding national legislation which enables the parties to an employment contract, without further conditions, to postpone the agreed termination of the employment relationship on reaching the standard retirement age for an unlimited period of time by agreement during the employment relationship, if necessary several times, merely because the employee is entitled to an old-age pension on reaching the standard retirement age?

4. the appeal proceedings are suspended until the Court of Justice of the European Union has ruled on the reference for a preliminary ruling.

Reasons

A. Subject-matter of the main proceedings

The parties are in dispute about the limitation of the employment relationship and claims to wages for default of acceptance.

The plaintiff, born on ... 1949, has been employed by the defendant as a salaried teacher for secondary level II since 2001.

Pursuant to § 2 of the employment contract concluded on 25 September 2001, the employment relationship is governed by the Federal Employees' Collective Agreement and the collective agreements supplementing, amending or replacing it in the version applicable to the Free Hanseatic City of Bremen. The Federal Employees' Collective Agreement has since been replaced by the Collective Agreement for the Public Service of the Federal States (hereinafter referred to as "TV-L").

In a letter dated 5 February 2014, the plaintiff applied for continued employment beyond the standard retirement age until the end of the 2015/2016 school year. On 24 October 2014, the parties concluded an agreement with the following content:

"The following agreement is concluded between ..., represented by ." and Mr H. J. born on ".1949 pursuant to Section 41 sentence 3 SGB VI in conjunction with. § 30 para. 1 sentence 1 TV-L: The automatic termination of the employment relationship of 31 July 2007 pursuant to § 44 No. 4 TV-L is postponed until 31 July 2015. The employment relationship shall end at the end of this date without the need for notice of termination. [.]"

In a letter dated 4 February 2015, the plaintiff again applied for continued employment until the end of the 2015/2016 school term. The defendant rejected this request in a letter dated 28 May 2015. The plaintiff contacted the defendant in a letter from his legal representative dated 16 June 2015 and pointed out that a time limit based on Section 41 sentence 3 SGB VI was inadmissible under European law. In a letter dated 27 July 2015, the defendant declared that the contractual relationship was effectively limited until 31 July 2015.

B. The relevant national law

§ Section 41 SGB VI in the version applicable since 23 June 2014 stipulates the following:

"Section 41 Old-age pension and protection against dismissal

...If an agreement provides for termination of the employment relationship upon reaching the standard retirement age, the parties to the employment contract may postpone the date of termination by agreement during the employment relationship, if necessary several times."

The relevant provisions in the collective agreement for the public service of the federal states are as follows: **"Section V - Fixed-term and termination of the employment relationship**

§ Section 30 Fixed-term employment contracts

(1) Fixed-term employment contracts are permitted on the basis of the Part-Time and Fixed-Term Employment Act and other statutory provisions on the limitation of employment contracts...

§ 44 TV-L Special regulations for employees as teaching staff

No. 4 to Section V - Fixed-term and termination of the employment relationship

The employment relationship shall end, without notice of termination being required, at the end of the school semester (31 January or 31 July) in which the teacher reaches the statutory retirement age."

C. Relevant provisions of Union law

§ Article 5(1) of the Framework Agreement on fixed-term work concluded on 18 March 1999, annexed to Council Directive 1999/70/EC of 28 June 1999 concerning the framework agreement on fixed-term work concluded by ETUC, UNICE and CEEP (OJ 1999 L 175, p. 43), reads as follows

"1. In order to prevent abuse arising from successive fixed-term work contracts or relationships, Member States shall, after consultation of the social partners as required by law or collective agreement or as is customary in the Member State, and/or the social partners where there are no equivalent legal measures to prevent abuse, take one or more of the following measures, taking into account the requirements of specific sectors and/or categories of workers:

(a) objective reasons justifying the extension of such contracts or relationships;

b) the maximum total authorised duration of successive employment contracts or relationships;

(c) the maximum number of renewals of such contracts or relationships.

(2) Member States, after consulting the social partners, and/or the social partners, as appropriate, shall determine the conditions under which fixed-term work contracts or employment relationships are

(a) are to be regarded as 'successive';

(b) are to be regarded as contracts or relationships of indefinite duration."

Articles 1, 2 and 6 of Council Directive 2000/78/EC of 27 November 2000 establishing a general framework for equal treatment in employment and occupation (Directive 2000/78/EC) read as follows:

Article 1

Purpose

The purpose of this Directive is to establish a general framework for combating discrimination on grounds of religion or belief, disability, age or sexual orientation in employment and occupation with a view to implementing the principle of equal treatment in the Member States.

Article 2

The concept of discrimination
(1. For the purposes of this Directive, the principle of equal treatment shall mean that there shall be no direct or indirect discrimination on any of the grounds referred to in Article 1.

(2. For the purposes of paragraph 1

(a) direct discrimination shall be taken to occur where one person is treated less favourably than another is, has been or would be treated in a comparable situation on any of the grounds referred to in Article 1

(b) indirect discrimination shall be taken to occur where an apparently neutral provision, criterion or practice may put persons of a particular religion or belief, disability, age or sexual orientation at a particular disadvantage compared with other persons, unless:

(i) those provisions, criteria or procedures are objectively justified by a legitimate aim and the means of achieving that aim are appropriate and necessary; or
(ii) the employer or any person or organisation to whom this Directive applies is required by national law, in the case of persons with a particular disability, to take appropriate measures in accordance with the principles set out in Article 5 to eliminate the disadvantages resulting from that provision, criterion or practice.

(3. Unwanted conduct which is related to one of the grounds referred to in Article 1 and which has the purpose or effect of violating the dignity of a person and of creating an intimidating, hostile, degrading, humiliating or offensive environment shall be harassment and shall be deemed to be discrimination within the meaning of paragraph 1. In this context, Member States may

define the term 'harassment' in accordance with national law and practice.

(4. An instruction to discriminate against a person on any of the grounds referred to in Article 1 shall be deemed to be discrimination within the meaning of paragraph 1.

(5. This Directive shall be without prejudice to measures provided for by national law which are necessary in a democratic society to safeguard public security, the defence of public order and the prevention of criminal offences, the protection of health and the protection of the rights and freedoms of others.

[...]

Article 6
Justified differences of treatment on grounds of age

1. Notwithstanding Article 2(2), Member States may provide that differences of treatment on grounds of age shall not constitute discrimination, provided that they are objective, proportionate and justified within the framework of national law by a legitimate aim, including in particular legitimate objectives relating to employment policy, the labour market and vocational training, and that the means of achieving that aim are appropriate and necessary.

Such unequal treatment may include in particular the following:

(a) the establishment of special conditions for access to employment and vocational training and special conditions of employment and work, including conditions of dismissal and remuneration, in order to promote the occupational integration of young people, older workers and persons with caring responsibilities or to ensure their protection;

(b) the establishment of minimum age, professional experience or length of service requirements for access to employment or for certain benefits linked to employment

(c) setting a maximum age for recruitment based on the specific training requirements of a particular job or on the need for an appropriate period of employment before retirement.

2. Notwithstanding Article 2(2), Member States may provide that, in occupational social security schemes, the setting of age limits as a condition for membership or receipt of retirement or invalidity benefits, including the setting of different age limits under such schemes for certain workers or groups or categories of workers, and the use under such schemes of age criteria for actuarial calculations, shall not constitute discrimination on grounds of age as long as it does not lead to discrimination on grounds of sex.

D. Necessity of the decision of the Court of Justice of the European Union and explanation of the question referred

The decision in the dispute depends on the interpretation of § 5 no. 1 of the framework agreement on fixed-term work concluded on 18 March 1999, annexed to Council Directive 1999/70/EC of 28 June 1999. Since in the present case there is no objective reason within the meaning of the Part-Time and Fixed-Term Employment Act for the agreement concluded between the parties on 14 October 2014, in which they postponed the termination of the employment relationship until 31 July 2015, the decisive question is whether Section 41 sentence 3 SGB VI as the legal basis of this agreement is compatible with Section 5 no. 1 of the framework agreement.

The scope of application of the framework agreement is relevant in the present case. The wording of § 2 no. 1 is broad, as it generally refers to "fixed-term employees with an employment contract or relationship as defined by law, collective agreement or practice in each Member State". The definition of the term "fixed-term worker" within the meaning of the Framework Agreement, which is contained in its § 3 No. 1, also covers all employees without distinguishing whether they are bound to a public or a private employer (ECJ 4 July 2006,

Adeneler and Others, C-212/04, EU:C:2006:443, para. 56; 13 March 2014, Marquez Samohano, C- 190/13, EU:C:2014:146, para. 38; 26 November 2014, Mascolo and Others, C-22/13, C-61/13, C63/13 and C-418/13, EU:C:2014:2401, para. 67). Nor does the Framework Agreement exclude any particular sector from its scope of application (CJEU 21 September 2016 - C614/15 -, para. 35).

It is therefore the task of the national court to review whether the national regulation fulfils the requirements set out in Section 5 of the Framework Agreement (ECJ 3 July 2014, Fiamingo et al, C-362/13, C-363/13 and C-407/13, EU:C:2014:2044, para. 66 and the case law cited therein, and of 26 November 2014, Mascolo and others, C-22/13, C- 61/13, C-63/13 and C-418/13, EU:C:2014:2401, para. 81; 21 September 2016 - C-614/15 -, para. 44, juris).

In the present case, the parties agreed in the employment contract of 30 July 2001 that the relevant collective agreements would apply. This means that, among other things, the provision of Section 44 No. 4 TV-L applies to the employment relationship, according to which the employment relationship ends at the end of the school semester in which the plaintiff has reached the statutory age for reaching a standard retirement pension without deductions. According to the above-mentioned principles, this is a fixed term. The postponement of this time limit in accordance with § 41 sentence 3 SGB VI accordingly constitutes an extension of this time limit, even if the wording of the law does not use the word extension but "postpone". According to the broad wording of the framework agreement, this situation is also subject to the regulations on fixed-term employment under EU law, as it is essentially an extension of the fixed-term employment relationship.

The application of the framework agreement in the present case is not precluded by the fact that the parties to the employment contract have only made use of the option under Section 41 sentence 3 SGB VI once. As this provision is in fact linked to the agreement in the employment contract, according to which the employment relationship ends when the standard retirement age is reached, it constitutes an extension of the fixed term agreed in the employment contract, so that the facts of multiple fixed terms are fulfilled.

§ Section 5(1) of the Framework Agreement aims to limit the repeated recourse to fixed-term employment contracts or relationships, which is seen as a source of potential abuse to the detriment of employees, by providing a series of minimum safeguards to prevent the precarisation of the situation of employees (ECJ 4 July 2006, Adeneler et al, C-212/04, EU:C:2006:443, para. 63, of 23 April 2009, Angelidaki and Others, C-378/07 to C-380/07, EU:C:2009:250, para. 73, of 26 January 2012, Kücük, C-586/10, EU:C:2012:39, para. 25, of 13 March 2014, Marquez Samohano, C-190/13, EU:C:2014:146, para. 41, of 3 July 2014, Fiamingo and Others, C-362/13, C-363/13 and C-407/13, EU:C:2014:2044, para. 54, and of 26 November 2014, Mascolou. a., C-22/13, C-61/13, C-63/13 and C-418/13, EU:C:2014:2401, para. 72).

It can be inferred from the second paragraph of the preamble to the Framework Agreement and from its General Recitals 6 and 8 that permanent employment relationships represent an important aspect of employee protection, whereas fixed-term employment contracts can only meet the needs of both employers and employees in certain circumstances (ECJ 4 July 2006, Adeneler and Others, C-212/04, EU:C:2006:443, para. 62, of 3 July 2014, Fiamingo and Others, C- 362/13, C-363/13 andC-407/13, EU:C:2014:2044, para. 55, and of 26 November 2014, Mascolo and Others, C-22/13, C-61/13, C-63/13 and C-418/13, EU:C:2014:2401, para. 73).

Therefore, in order to prevent the abusive use of successive fixed-term employment contracts or relationships, § 5 no. 1 of the Framework Agreement obliges the Member States to take at least one of the measures listed therein effectively and with binding effect if their national law does not contain equivalent statutory measures. Section 41 sentence 3 SGB VI does not fulfil these requirements, as none of the three measures listed in Section 5 no. 1 letters a to c are listed in this provision. These measures relate in detail to objective reasons that justify the extension of such employment contracts or relationships, the overall maximum permissible duration of these successive employment contracts or relationships and the permissible number of their extensions (see ECJ 23 April 2009, Angelidaki and others, C-378/07 to C-380/07, EU:C:2009:250, para. 74, of 26 January 2012, Kücük, C-586/10,

EU:C:2012:39, para. 26, of 13 March 2014, Marquez Samohano, C-190/13, EU:C:2014:146, para. 42, of 3 July 2014, Fiamingo et al, C-362/13, C-363/13 and C-407/13, EU:C:2014:2044, para. 56, and of 26 November 2014, Mascolo and Others, C-22/13, C-61/13, C- 63/13and C-418/13, EU:C:2014:2401, para. 74; 21 September 2016 - C-614/15).

In contrast, Section 41 sentence 3 SGB VI allows the agreed termination of the employment relationship to be postponed several times upon reaching the standard retirement age without any time restrictions. The ECJ has already established that § 5 no. 1 of the framework agreement precludes the use of successive fixed-term employment contracts which is justified solely by the fact that it is provided for in a general legal provision of a Member State (ECJ 4 July 2006 - C-212/04 - Adeneler).

In justifying the provision in Section 41 sentence 3 SGB VI, the national legislator, following on from the ECJ ruling of 21 July 2011, stated that by postponing the termination date beyond the standard retirement age, employees and employers can react, for example, if the position in question cannot be filled seamlessly. Employees could also use their expertise to successfully complete ongoing projects or familiarise newly hired, younger colleagues with their work (BT-Drs. 18/1489 p. 25).

The Chamber questions whether these fundamentally legitimate objectives cited by the national legislator require a deviation from Section 5 No. 1 of the Framework Agreement in order to avoid the abuse of multiple fixed-term contracts or whether such a deviation appears appropriate.

The socio-political objective of an employment distribution between the generations (cf. ECJ 12 October 2010 Rosenbladt loc. cit.) is not made impossible by postponing the termination of the employment relationship after reaching the standard retirement age, but it is delayed. The possibility cited by the national legislator as justification for § 41 sentence 3 SGB VI to enable the induction of a younger employee by postponing the termination of the employment relationship upon reaching the standard retirement age is, in the view of the Chamber, only of minor practical significance.

significance. As the employer knows the age of his employee and therefore knows when the employment relationship will end when the standard retirement age is reached, he regularly has sufficient time to find a suitable successor in good time and to have him trained. Conversely, training by the departing employee is out of the question if a successor has not yet been found at the time of departure. In practice, it is therefore only necessary to postpone the termination of the employment relationship within the meaning of Section 41 sentence 3 SGB VI in a case where the employer only finds a successor for the departing employee so shortly before the departing employee reaches the standard retirement age that the departing employee does not have sufficient time to familiarise their successor before the employment relationship ends. However, this case constellation does not require a deviation from § 5 No. 1 of the framework agreement. The familiarisation of a subsequent employee is - 11 - regularly limited in time. There are therefore no factual indications for the Chamber as to why a multiple fixed-term option without a time limit should be necessary for such familiarisation.

The same applies to the case constellation in which the employer has not yet found a suitable successor at the time of the employee's contractual departure. If the termination of the employment relationship is postponed in order to find a suitable successor so that the departing employee can still be trained, this situation also does not require an unlimited time limit.

The further purpose stated by the national legislator, according to which postponing the termination of the employment relationship upon reaching the standard retirement age opens up the possibility for an employee to complete a project, does not, in the view of the Chamber, require a special provision within the meaning of Section 41 sentence 3 SGB VI that deviates from Section 5 no. 1 of the framework agreement, since the fixed-term project constitutes a material reason within the meaning of Section 14 para. 1 no. 1 TzBfG.

There is also a lack of an equivalent statutory measure that effectively and deterrently guarantees the objective pursued by Section 5 No. 1 of the framework agreement of preventing the abuse of multiple fixed-term contracts.

In view of the unambiguous wording of the law, the Chamber considers itself prevented from interpreting Section 41 sentence 3 SGB VI in accordance with EU law. The principle of interpretation in conformity with EU law cannot form the basis for an interpretation of national law contra legem (see ECJ 8 November 2016 - C-554/14 -, para. 66; 16 June 2005, Pupino, C-105/03, EU:C:2005:386, para. 47; 5 September 2012, Lopes Da Silva Jorge, C-42/11, EU:C:2012:517, paras. 55 and 56). The Member States have discretionary powers when transposing EU law. In the present case, when drafting Section 41 sentence 3 SGB VI, the national legislator had the choice of relying on one or more of the measures listed in Section 5 no. 1 a to c or on existing equivalent statutory measures, taking into account the requirements of certain sectors and/or categories of employees (see ECJ 3 July 2014, Fiamingou. a., C-362/13, C363/13 and C-407/13, EU:C:2014:2044, para. 59 and the case law cited therein, and of 26 November 2014, Mascolo and Others, C-22/13, C-61/13, C-63/13 and C-418/13, EU:C:2014:2401, para. 75; 21 September 2016 - C- 614/15 -, para. 39, juris). In contrast, the Chamber does not have such a discretion. The fact that the national legislator has not exercised its discretion in conformity with Union law does not give the Chamber the possibility, in the context of an interpretation in conformity with Union law, to exercise a discretion contra legem in place of the legislator and to limit the unrestricted possibility of extending the time limit within the meaning of § 5 no. 1 of the Framework Agreement pursuant to § 41 sentence 3 SGB VI.

Where, as in the present case, EU law does not provide for specific sanctions in the event that abuses have been identified, it is for the national authorities to take measures which must not only be proportionate but also effective and dissuasive enough to ensure the full effectiveness of the standards adopted to implement the framework agreement (CJEU 3 July 2014, Fiamingo and Others, C-362/13, C-363/13 and C-407/13, EU:C:2014:2044, para. 62 and the case law cited therein, and of

26 November 2014, Mascolo and Others, C-22/13, C- 61/13, C-63/13 and C-418/13, EU:C:2014:2401, para. 77; 21 September 2016 - C- 614/15).

The need to ensure the full effectiveness of a prohibition of a directive therefore means in the present case that the Chamber either does not apply Section 41 sentence 3 SGB VI or requests a preliminary ruling from the Court of Justice.

In the Chamber's view, it is necessary to clarify the question of whether the measures prescribed in § 5 no. 1 of the Framework Agreement are necessary in the present case in view of the purpose pursued by the Framework Agreement. The European Court of Justice has not yet interpreted the compatibility of § 41 sentence 3 SGB VI. If the purpose of the directive is to prevent abusive multiple fixed-term contracts in order to prevent the precarisation of an employment relationship, the question arises as to whether such precarisation is relevant in the present case constellation, in which the employee has reached the standard limit for the statutory entitlement to an old-age pension. The Court of Justice has established that clauses on the automatic termination of the employment relationship when the employee reaches retirement age should not, in principle, be regarded as unduly prejudicial to the legitimate interests of the employees concerned (ECJ 12 October 2010 - C-45/09 - [Rosenbladt] para. 47).

In the Chamber's view, the question of whether the measures prescribed in § 5 no. 1 of the framework agreement could be dispensable for the present case constellation because the provision of § 41 sentence 3 SGB VI enables an employee to remain in the employment relationship who would otherwise have to leave the employment relationship is also in need of clarification. The provision of Section 41 sentence 3 SGB VI could also be interpreted in such a way that it mitigates the forcing out of older employees from the employment relationship by limiting the employment relationship to the standard retirement age. An employee who reaches the standard age for drawing a statutory old-age pension is not only different from other employees in terms of social security, but also in that he is regularly at the end of his working life and is therefore not faced with the alternative of an otherwise permanent employment relationship with regard to the time limit, but rather the termination of the employment relationship is regularly associated with the end of active working life as a whole and thus entry into retirement.

The interpretation of Council Directive 2000/78/EC of 27 November 2000 establishing a general framework for equal treatment in employment and occupation (Directive 2000/78/EC) is also relevant to the resolution of the legal dispute.

The Court of Justice has already established that clauses on the automatic termination of the employment relationship when the employee reaches retirement age are not, in principle, to be regarded as unduly prejudicial to the legitimate interests of the employees concerned (ECJ 12 October 2010 - C-45/09 - [Rosenbladt] para. 47). Such a provision is not only based on a certain age, but also takes into account the fact that the persons concerned are entitled to financial compensation at the end of their professional career in the form of income replacement in the form of a retirement pension (see ECJ 21 July 2011 - C-159/10 and C-160/10 - [Fuchs] para. 64 et seq., EzA EC Treaty 1999 Directive 2000/78 No. 20; 12 October 2010 - C-45/09 - [Rosenbladt] para. 48, loc. cit.). According to the case law of the Court of Justice, it is therefore "not unreasonable" for the authorities of a Member State to assume that a measure such as the admissibility stipulated in § 10 sentence 3 no. 5 AGG could be appropriate and necessary in order to achieve the legitimate objectives of national labour and employment policy (ECJ 12 October 2010 - C-45/09 - [Rosenbladt] para. 51, loc. cit.; cf. in this sense already 16 October 2007 - C-411/05 - [Palacios de la Villa] para. 72, ECR 2007, I-8531).

In the present case, the Chamber questions whether the justifications for the termination of the employment relationship upon reaching the standard retirement age can also be applied to the extension of such a fixed term. The socio-political objective of a distribution of employment between the generations (cf. ECJ 12 October 2010 Rosenbladt loc. cit.) is, as already explained, not achieved by postponing the termination of the employment relationship after reaching the standard retirement age.

employment relationship after reaching the standard retirement age is not made impossible, but it is delayed.

However, the purpose of § 41 sentence 3 SGB VI can also be understood as mitigating the forcing out of older employees from the employment relationship by limiting the employment relationship to when they reach the standard retirement age. Unlike younger employees, an employee who reaches the standard retirement age is regularly faced with the alternative of extending this employment relationship or retiring completely.

Declaration of self-employment

I hereby declare,

(surname, first name)

that I have written this thesis independently and without outside help and have not used any aids other than those specified. In particular, I declare that I have labelled all verbatim and analogous references from other works as such.

(Place, date) (Signature)

FSC
www.fsc.org
MIX
Papier | Fördert gute Waldnutzung
FSC® C083411

Kolibri 360 GmbH
Ferdinand-Jühlke-Straße 7
99095 Erfurt, Deutschland
produktsicherheit@kolibri360.de

Druck:
CPI Druckdienstleistungen GmbH
im Auftrag der
Kolibri 360 GmbH
Ferdinand-Jühlke-Str. 7
99095 Erfurt